Leaders
Attitude, Behaviour & Action

Leaders
Attitude, Behaviour & Action

Shahana

Dedicated to my Father & Mother

Content

Acknowledge

Welcome note

Preface

Author Note

Introduction

Chapter 1: "Leadership: A Natural Aspect of Caregiving, Where Visionaries Shape the Future"

Chapter 2: Leaders Who Transform by Choice, not by Title

Chapter 3: Leaders Show Gratitude

Chapter 4: Competition and Comparison are not on the list

Chapter 5: Reflection on Action: The Essence of True Leadership

Chapter 6: The Leadership Equation: Comfort, Space, and Recognition

Chapter 7: Leading with Emotional Intelligence

Chapter 8: Collaboration and Inclusivity: Fostering a Culture of Belonging

Chapter 9: Self-care as leadership

Chapter 10: Leaders are not ordinary, they make Extraordinary choices

Chapter 11: I don't know

Chapter 12: Freedom to Fail

Recollecting

Reference

Acknowledge

I have an abundance of gratitude for the amazing life I enjoy, which is a result of the encouraging leaders who have created a space where my ideas and opinions are allowed to freely grow. I have long adored the idea of working in such a loving atmosphere, and I am deeply indebted to all who have been instrumental in my journey.

Above all, Farhana, my sister, has been a constant source of support for me at every turn in my life. My friend Chhaya Saxena her confidence in me and her support have been my biggest strengths. Following that, I must thank Surya Banshi for the review & Suggestion., he is a quiet but influential leader who has listened with patience. My friend Mamoon has been an incredible source of support in my life.

I would especially want to thank Vishwas Pandey for his insightful thoughts on leadership, which have had an impact on my perception of leadership as something I have experienced. Undoubtedly, my sincere gratitude also goes out to my Deoria-based Jagriti teammates, Naina Verma, Dhirendra Yadav, Shubham Tripathi, Vikas Shahi, and Vivek Vishwakarma. Since my arrival, their support and companionship have been a continual source of strength. Anand Singh for giving me suggestions for a book cover.

I would like to express heartfelt gratitude to my family, specifically Sushmita, Mantasha, and Imran. These incredible individuals have played an integral role in shaping and beautifying my journey.

At the Last Zakat Foundation of India, it's only because of this organisation I am who I am.

<u>Welcome note</u>

Dear readers,

Have you ever thought about what it means to be a leader? I sure have. "Leadership is not about being in charge. It's about taking care of those in your charge." - Simon Sinek

In this book, I want to share some real-life leaders' stories and what we all read somewhere. I think of leadership as a coin with two sides: being the BOSS and being the LEADER. We all have both of these sides within us, and it's up to us to choose which one to embrace.

Developing exceptional leadership skills is a challenging yet rewarding journey that demands a deep level of commitment, empathy, and respect for others. We can create a positive and constructive environment that fosters growth and success by nurturing and supporting those around us. Through our actions, we can inspire and motivate others to become the best version of themselves.

Throughout these pages, I want to talk about how the decisions we make shape our journey as leaders and impact others. True leadership comes when we practise gratitude, especially when things get tough.

It's about helping others see the good in life, even during hard times, and giving them the courage to find their paths with strength and resilience.

Cheers,

Shahana

Preface

Leadership is an ancient concept which evolved through the contributions of various thinkers, scholars, and practitioners from diverse fields and cultures.

Leadership is a complicated phenomenon that has attracted the attention of scholars from diverse fields, including psychology, sociology, and organisational behaviour. Over the years, these scholars have worked tirelessly to develop theories and frameworks to better understand this concept. In particular, the contributions of renowned figures such as *Max Weber* (German sociologist), who introduced the idea of charismatic leadership, and *Kurt Lewin* (German-American psychologist), who is famous for his work on leadership styles, have significantly influenced the study of leadership. Dr. B.R. Ambedkar played a big role in making the Indian Constitution and was an important leader during India's fight for independence. He strongly believed in making sure everyone is treated fairly and equally, especially those who are often left out or ignored. His ideas have influenced how people think about leadership, especially when making positive changes and including everyone in the process.

Their groundbreaking work has provided valuable insights into the nature of leadership and has contributed to the development of more effective leadership practices in various settings.

Throughout human history, leadership has been an integral part of communal living. In ancient tribes, individuals naturally assumed leadership roles by tending to the needs of their community, ensuring survival, and fostering unity. This innate inclination towards leadership persists today.

In ancient societies, leaders emerged based on their ability to provide protection, make decisions for the group, and guide them through challenges. These leaders were often respected members of the community who demonstrated qualities such as *empathy, courage, wisdom, honesty and the ability to inspire others.* As societies evolved, so did the concept of leadership. With the advent of agriculture, trade, and civilisation, leadership structures became more complex, ranging from tribal chieftains and monarchs to elected officials and appointed leaders. However, the core principles of leadership—responsibility, service, and influence—remained constant.

Fast forward to today, where we find ourselves in an increasingly technologically advanced world driven by artificial intelligence (AI). While AI has revolutionised many aspects of our lives, the essence of leadership remains relevant. Just as ancient leaders cared for their tribes, modern leaders must navigate the complexities of our interconnected global community, address societal challenges, and inspire collective action.

In this AI-driven world, leadership takes on new dimensions. Leaders must harness the power of technology responsibly, making decisions that prioritise the well-being of both people and the planet. They must also adapt to rapid changes, foster innovation, and cultivate diverse and inclusive environments where everyone can thrive.

Despite these advancements, the fundamental principles of leadership endure. Whether it's a fourth-grader looking after a friend or a CEO guiding a multinational corporation, leadership is ultimately about serving others, inspiring positive change, and leaving a lasting impact on the world. As we navigate the complexities of the AI era, the timeless qualities of effective leadership—empathy, integrity, vision, and resilience—will continue to shape our collective journey forward.

Author Note

As a writer passionate about discovering human potential, I firmly believe that leadership is a quality that exists inside every person, outside the walls of authority. It's a concept I'm fascinated by sharing: that every one of us represents the two sides of a coin, capable of adopting the role of either Boss or Leader. In the end, it is up to us to decide.

Being a leader requires a deliberate journey filled with efforts to uplift and nourish those around us, as well as a conscious commitment to empathy and respect. It's a difficult but incredibly gratifying task that calls for us to handle the complexities of interpersonal relationships with dignity and honour.

I hope to shed light on the transformational impact of our decisions in forming our leadership journeys inside the pages of this book. I want readers to explore the minor but significant differences between accepting leadership and rejecting the influence of authority through thought-provoking writings and sad stories. Great leadership emerges when people deliberately practise gratefulness in the face of hardship, encouraging others to see the beauty in life's situations and giving them the confidence to choose their pathways with grace and resiliency.

Introduction

Have you ever wondered what true leadership is all about? There is a basic truth to be found in the middle of our hectic lives, among the daily setbacks and triumphs: being a leader is a choice we make daily, not merely a label that is bestowed upon us.

A choice to be a boss or a leader is a conscious decision we make with every action. When I was learning about leadership I used to imagine that I was a perfect example of a leader but when I stepped into the world of leaders I realised I was practising a boss role. It is not easy when we are all aware of everything thanks to the internet but we are disconnecting with the practices.

All too frequently, we mistake being in charge with being a leader. True leadership goes beyond simple authority, even though the label of "boss" may come with power and control. It has to do with impact, inspiration, and influence. It involves providing direction with compassion, wisdom, and vision.

We explore the important reality that leadership is a choice in this book. We all grasp this coin in our hands and are aware of its importance and weight. Shall we turn it over to the "Boss" side, where orders and directions rule? Alternatively, should we tread the road of the "Leader," where our behaviour is defined by empowerment, teamwork, and service?

In the pages that follow, we shall talk about the subtleties of this choice. We'll talk about the qualities that surpass a job title and distinguish a great leader from a manager. We will learn from the stories of those who have acknowledged their inner leadership and the beneficial impacts they have had on their organisations, businesses, and society as a whole.

Join me on this enlightening and self-exploration adventure. Let's embrace the leader that is inside every one of us and together flip the leadership coin. It is in this decision that not only will we succeed but also the advancement and welfare of all those under our leadership.

Chapter 1

Leadership: A Natural Aspect of Caregiving, Where Visionaries Shape the Future

Care

Eleventh President of India and renowned scientist Dr APJ Abdul Kalam has discussed the attributes of a successful leader, among them the significance of *empathy*. He held that a leader needs to have empathy and compassion for the people they are in charge of in addition to vision and resolve.
"A leader should be a visionary and a listener. But most importantly, a leader should be a nurturer of dreams, caring for the aspirations of those around him." APJ Abdul Kalam

In the same way, Mr Shashank Mani Tripathi's strategy fits this idea of caring leadership.

When I sought advice from Mr Shashank Mani Tripathi, founder of Jagriti Yatra and Jagriti Enterprise, on teaching leadership skills to a fourth-grader during his book reading session (Middle of Daimond India), he provided a simple yet profound approach. Mr Tripathi's suggestion was straightforward: assigning the child the responsibility of looking after a friend seated nearby. This idea resonates deeply with a fundamental aspect of leadership—the duty to care for and support others. It illustrates how leadership is not just about authority but also about empathy, responsibility, and communal harmony, reflecting the timeless essence of leadership across cultures and generations.

In ancient times, when people lived in small groups, leaders were very important. They were like the protectors and decision-makers for the group. These leaders were respected because they were kind, brave, smart, and could inspire others. As time went on and people started farming and trading, leadership became more complicated. Some leaders were like chiefs in tribes, others were kings or queens of big kingdoms. They all had different jobs but they were all expected to be responsible, helpful, and have the power to make good things happen for everyone.

Even today, the idea of what makes a good leader hasn't changed much. We still want leaders who are responsible, who care about others, and who can make things better. So, whether it's a class project or leading a big country, the important qualities of a leader stay the same: being kind, taking care of others, and being someone who can make good decisions for everyone.

Visualisation

Prominent media personality Oprah Winfrey often talks about how powerful it is to visualise your dreams. She says it's like painting a picture of the future you want, especially for leaders. When you visualise, you imagine your ideal job or a successful project. It's not just daydreaming – Oprah believes it's a way to make your ideas come true! By picturing success, you can inspire others and overcome challenges. It's like having a superpower! Oprah advises leaders to practise visualising every day to achieve their goals. So, leaders, grab your mental paintbrush and start dreaming big!

In my chat with Mr Shashank at Jagriti Enterprise, the genius behind Jagriti Yatra, I asked about the origins of this incredible journey. "How did you even think of Jagriti Yatra? You know, that awesome trip where 500 people travel, meet entrepreneurs, and learn, not compete," I asked. Mr Shashank's answer showed the power of visualisation. He told me how he used to imagine bringing people from all over the world to his village. He pictured them by a big tree, hugging it and all. This was way before he knew how it could happen. And guess what? In 2008, his dream came true with Jagriti Yatra. Just like Oprah says, Mr. Shashank's story shows how believing in your dreams and visualising them can make amazing things happen!

So, leaders don't just think, they dream big and make it happen. It's pretty amazing, right? They imagine things that don't even exist yet, and then they work hard to turn those dreams into reality. It's like having a superpower! And Jagriti Yatra? It's not just a trip, it's a journey of discovery. People come together, not to compete, but to learn from each other and grow together. That's the kind of leader Mr. Shashank is – someone who sees possibilities where others see challenges.

So, if you ever have a big dream, remember Mr. Shashank and how he turned his vision into the world's largest entrepreneurial journey. Who knows? Maybe you'll be the next big leader with a dream that changes the world!

Chapter 2

Leaders Who Transform by Choice, not by Title

I became interested in the idea of leadership throughout my early school years. I recall seeing those classmates who were often invited to take part in extracurricular activities or assigned responsibilities like gathering notebooks. It made me wonder: Is a leader someone who is always being asked to do more and given more responsibility by others? This question followed me during my time at college, when I too saw students in leadership roles occasionally acting aggressively and controllingly.

However, my perspective on leadership underwent a profound transformation when I became part of the Gandhi Fellowship. The Fellowship assigned each group of 4 to 5 fellows a Program Leader (PL), and it was during my time in Bihar from 2019 to 2021 that I truly started to grasp the essence of leadership.

In Sitamarhi, Bihar, I had the privilege of working under the guidance of three remarkable Program Leaders: Sonali Sapna, Kundan Kumar, and Arvind Kumar. These individuals were not merely leaders by title; they embodied the very spirit of leadership.

I learned from their excellent behaviour that a leader is someone who prioritises the welfare of their team above all else. Sonali, Kundan, and Arvind never disregarded anyone since they saw the potential in everyone. These leaders united us and created a single front despite our differences in perspective and background.

Working alongside 16 fellows in a challenging locale, Sonali, Kundan, and Arvind crafted a nurturing environment where feedback wasn't just welcomed—it was actively sought. An open-door policy prevailed, ensuring that anyone could voice their thoughts, and assured they would be heard and valued.

Our days start with Baal Geet, children's songs that set a harmonious tone for the day ahead. As each day wound down, we gathered for a reflective debrief, a cherished ritual where we shared our top emotions. This practice solidified our team bond and enabled us to support one another through the highs and lows of our journey.

As I think back on my experiences, I've realised that being a leader involves much more than just being in a position of power. It's about living up to a set of ideals and standards that motivate, empower, and encourage others around us. Seeing the leadership philosophies of people like Sonali, Kundan, and Arvind—whose methods have served as inspiration for me in my leadership development—has greatly influenced my viewpoint.

Sonali helped me understand the value of trusting in one's team by providing me with tough yet compassionate coaching. She had a special ability to give each team member confidence, making us feel important and competent. Her style of leadership was one of cooperation and trust-building rather than giving commands. I recall how she urged us to express our opinions, regardless of how strange they might sound. We produced amazing outcomes together thanks to this strategy, which fostered a creative atmosphere.

In the same manner, Kundan's leadership style was characterised by his constant encouragement and support. He had a talent for seeing and developing people's potential. I remember a moment when I questioned my skills, but Kundan never lost faith in me. He pushed me to grow and challenge myself by offering advice and mentoring. He created an environment where I felt comfortable taking chances and learning from mistakes through his leadership, which was a mix of friendliness and mentoring.

Arvind, however, was a perfect example of how effective open communication and openness can be in a leadership role. He thought it was crucial to include everyone in the decision-making process and to keep them informed. We didn't feel like followers, but rather like important participants because of Arvind's inclusive style. I recall how he would get us together for frequent team meetings so that everyone could voice their opinions. We had a common purpose that drove us towards our objectives because of this sense of ownership and participation.

These encounters have taught me that true leadership entails fostering a climate of cooperation, trust, and support. It all comes down to having faith in each person's ability and giving them the resources and support they need to reach their goals. My leadership style is based on the leadership philosophies of Sonali, Kundan, and Arvind.

I am appreciative of the progress and lessons I have learnt as I reflect on my path. By educating people about the transforming potential of genuine leadership, I aim to return the favour. Not only is it a grand ideal, but leadership that uplifts, empowers, and brings out the best in everyone is a genuine thing that can transform the world for the better.

These encounters have taught me that true leadership entails fostering a culture of support.

By sharing my experiences, I hope to shed light on the way to a leadership approach that is compassionate, inclusive, and genuinely transformative. We can build situations where everyone feels heard, respected, and encouraged to realise their full potential if we adopt these values, in my opinion. I want to positively impact the lives of those around me by promoting a culture of success, development, and cooperation through the lens of authentic leadership.

Chapter 3

Leaders Show Gratitude

Thanking god for a meal both before and after eating may have felt like a basic etiquette to us as kids. However, the value of appreciation only increases with age, particularly in the context of leadership. Why is it that leaders always stress the importance of having gratitude?

The Impact of Gratitude & Appreciation

Gratitude plays a crucial role in this process by fostering positive relationships, enhancing team morale, and increasing productivity. Research conducted by Harvard Business Review (Smith, 2020) suggests that leaders who express gratitude towards their team members create a culture of appreciation, leading to higher job satisfaction and employee motivation.

Moreover, thankfulness increases team trust. A leader may foster a sense of loyalty and togetherness by thanking individuals for their contributions. This was demonstrated in a study published in the Journal of Personality and Social Psychology (Jones et al., 2018), which discovered a positive correlation between team member trust and leadership thankfulness.

Mr Anurag Dixit, the Chief Operating Officer (COO) of JECP (Jagriti Enterprise Centre Purvanchal). He's not just any boss; he's an incredible leader who pays attention to every little thing his team does, no matter how small. Imagine if you were in a team and your leader always noticed and said "thank you" for your efforts – that's Mr. Anurag! What's special about Mr. Anurag is that he creates a happy and positive place for everyone at JECP to work. When someone does something good, no matter how tiny, he makes sure they know it's appreciated. This makes everyone feel important and valued, which is super important in a team.

Impact of Gratitude on the Culture of the Organisation

Gratitude can influence an organisation's culture on a larger scale than only interpersonal relationships. Gratitude is a basic characteristic of leaders, and they create a favourable atmosphere in the workplace. A more engaged workforce results from employees feeling appreciated and respected. According to research that was published in the Journal of Applied Psychology (Chen et al., 2019), organisations that foster a culture of thankfulness have fewer employee turnover and better levels of well-being.

Moreover, thankfulness might help strengthen resilience during challenging situations. When team leaders show thankfulness even in the face of adversity, it inspires hope and determination in their members. This was emphasised in a study published in the Journal of Business Ethics (Garcia, 2017), which covered how leaders who showed thankfulness at trying times observed improvements in their team's cohesiveness and capacity for problem-solving.

Let's see an exercise to build a better culture in the organisation:

Exercise: Gratitude Circle

Objective: To promote a culture of gratitude and appreciation within the organisation, fostering positive relationships, teamwork, and enthusiasm among team members.

Facilitation Steps:

Introduction (5 minutes)
- Gather the team in a circle.
- Welcome everyone and explain the purpose of the Gratitude Circle.
- Emphasise that this exercise is about fostering a culture of appreciation and positivity within the team.

Setting the Tone (2 minutes)

- Share a brief example of something
  you're grateful for related to work or
  a colleague.
- This sets the tone and encourages
  others to follow suit.

Gratitude Sharing (15 minutes)
- Start with the facilitator (you) to
  model the activity.
- Then, invite the person to your left to
  share something they're grateful for
  at work.
- Each person continues around the
  circle.
- Encourage specific examples, such
  as a recent achievement, support
  from a coworker, or a positive
  experience.

Active Listening (10 minutes)
- As each team member shares, others
  in the circle listen attentively.
- Encourage non-verbal cues of
  support, such as nodding or smiling.
- Remind participants to refrain from
  interrupting while someone else is
  speaking.

Expressing Appreciation (10 minutes)

- After each person shares, invite others in the circle to express appreciation.
- This can be as simple as saying "thank you" or offering a positive comment.
- Ensure everyone has a chance to receive gratitude and support from their colleagues.

Rotation (10 minutes)
- Continue around the circle until all team members have had an opportunity to share.
- If the group is large, consider breaking into smaller circles to allow for more intimate interactions.
- Monitor time to ensure everyone gets a chance to participate.

Reflection and Action (5 minutes)
- Conclude the activity with a brief reflection period.
- Ask team members to think about how they can incorporate more gratitude into their daily interactions.
- Encourage them to take action by expressing appreciation through emails, notes, or verbal recognition.

Closing (3 minutes)

- Thank everyone for participating in the Gratitude Circle.
- Emphasise the importance of continuing to express gratitude in the workplace.
- Optionally, invite feedback on the activity and suggestions for future sessions.

Benefits

1. The Gratitude Circle fosters open communication and stronger bonds, enhancing team cohesion.

2. Focusing on gratitude boosts positivity, improves morale, and supports team building, leading to increased employee retention.

Chapter 4

Competition and Comparison are not on the list

Leadership doesn't welcome competition or comparison. Instead, it's about inspiring and guiding people toward a common goal. A good leader shares authority within their group, helping out and cheering others on when needed. They create a space where different ideas are welcomed, and teamwork is key.

Trust and being truthful are super important in leadership. A leader sticks to their values and helps their team members grow. Most importantly, leadership is about helping others, putting their needs first, and working for the greater good.

Growing this kind of mindset without competition or comparison needs a safe and supportive environment. Since we're little kids, we're surrounded by a culture that likes competition and comparison. Like in childhood, we rush to finish our food first, do better than our siblings, or try to be the best at school. To develop good leadership skills, it takes a whole community. Together, we need to be aware of how our words and actions shape this mindset. When we work together like this, we build a culture that values teamwork, respects different ideas, and focuses on honesty and trust. This kind of environment not only helps create strong leaders but also helps everyone grow and become better.

Leaders avoid competition and comparison because true leadership is about bringing people together, not setting them against each other. When a leader competes with their team members, it creates a negative environment where people might feel stressed or not valued. Instead, leaders focus on motivating and guiding everyone towards a common goal.

Comparing people can also lead to jealousy and resentment, which can harm teamwork. A good leader knows that every person is unique and brings something special to the team. They value these differences and encourage collaboration rather than competition.

By avoiding competition and comparison, leaders can create a positive and supportive atmosphere where everyone can thrive. This allows each team member to focus on their strengths and contribute their best to the group without worrying about outdoing others.

The most important thing is how we can eliminate comparison and competition while working with a large team. Working with people we tend to compare the capacity of one person with another person people don't speak up openly but somewhere it goes inside the head.

The strategies shared below are from principles of effective team leadership, collaboration, and organisational psychology, as well as best practices from industry leaders and management literature such as "Dare to Lead" by Brené Brown and "The Culture Code" by Daniel Coyle.

1. Encourage a Culture of Collaboration: Prioritise group success and common objectives over individual accomplishment to foster a culture of teamwork. Provide your team members the chance to work together on projects and exchange ideas to promote harmony and cooperation.

2. Define Roles and Responsibilities Clearly: To reduce uncertainty and the possibility of comparison, clearly state each team member's position and responsibilities. Make sure that everyone is aware of how their contributions complement one another and fit into the larger scheme.

3. Highlight Individual qualities: Acknowledge and value each team member's distinct abilities and qualities. Instead of comparing oneself to others, encourage people to use

their strengths to further the success of the team.

4. Promote Open Communication: Create an atmosphere where team members are at ease sharing their ideas, opinions, and worries. To encourage cooperation and understanding, give constructive criticism and practise active listening.

5. Celebrate Diversity: Appreciate the range of viewpoints, experiences, and backgrounds that exist within the team. Understand that varying points of view can enliven conversations and inspire more creative solutions.

6. Encourage team members to emphasise their personal development instead of comparing themselves to other people. To encourage personal development, offer chances for mentorship, training, and skill-building.

7. Establish team objectives: Set attainable, measurable goals that will require cooperation and teamwork to achieve. Stress the value of cooperating to achieve shared goals as opposed to conflict with one another.

8. Lead by Example: As a leader, exhibit cooperative behaviour by creating a welcoming and inclusive team atmosphere.

Refrain from favouritism and from setting teammates against one another.

9. Deal with Conflict Right Away: When situations of rivalry or comparison occur inside the team, deal with them quickly and respectfully. Promote frank discussion as a means of resolving disputes and emphasise the value of teamwork.

10. Encourage a Growth Mindset: Rather than clinging to rigid ideas of success or failure, foster a growth-oriented mindset that emphasises learning and progress. Reiterate that everyone can advance their knowledge and abilities through time.

Remember if you are working in a group or as a team and your leaders start comparison, just leave it's a wrong number. You cannot grow there ever.

Chapter 5

Reflection on Action: The Essence of True Leadership

Leaders are those who bring qualities of reflection for themself as well as for their team. Let us understand and explore a different side of leadership.

What does it mean to reflect on action? Well, imagine this: you're in a situation where a decision needs to be made. It could be something as simple as choosing a team project or as complex as handling a conflict. Instead of jumping right in with the first idea that comes to mind, reflecting on action means taking a moment to pause and think.

Let's break it down. When you reflect on action, you're looking back at what you've done - whether it's a successful project, a challenging conversation, or even a mistake. You as a leader ask yourself & team questions like What worked well? What could have been better? How do actions impact others? This type of reflection isn't about fixating on the past or criticizing for mistakes. It's about learning and growing from our experiences.

Now, here's where the magic happens - when you apply this reflection not just to yourself, but to your team as well. As a leader, you're not just responsible for your actions; you're also guiding and supporting your team. Encouraging your team members to reflect on their actions can lead to incredible growth and development.

Imagine this scenario: your team just completed a project, and it didn't go as smoothly as planned. Instead of pointing fingers or getting frustrated, you gather everyone together for a reflection session. You ask questions like What went well during the project? What challenges did we face? How can we improve next time? This kind of reflection creates a safe space for open and honest discussion. It allows everyone to share their thoughts and ideas without fear of judgment. This I have seen while working as a Gandhi Fellow as well as in JECP. During Gandhi fellowship When we were in PSL Rajasthan For the induction program. After the day ended, the facilitator of the session used to take feedback from us. What went right in the session and what Could be better next time to make everyone clear and give better learning? In Jagriti After a workshop CEO Mr Ashutosh & COO Mr Anurag used to take feedback from a team about what went right and what we can do better next time. As a leader, they never criticised us but encouraged us. Reflection is a core skill of a leader which they practise very carefully. These two major questions may sound so simple but trust me the outcome does wonders.

Peter Senge, a prominent organizational theorist and author of "The Fifth Discipline," emphasises the concept of "learning organisations." Senge advocates for continuous learning and improvement within teams and organizations. He highlights the importance of reflection on action as a means to identify systemic patterns, learn from past experiences, and adapt to change effectively.

Accepting reflection on action as a young leader may have a significant effect on the dynamics within your team. It fosters a culture of innovation and continuous improvement. Members of a team are more inclined to share their finest ideas and cooperate to achieve a common objective when they feel respected and heard.

However, contemplation of action involves more than simply looking back; it also involves looking forward. It involves applying the knowledge gained from previous encounters to choices and deeds made in the future. What distinguishes excellent leaders is their forward-thinking approach.

Let's now discuss the advantages of action-reflection. It mostly encourages self-awareness. By pausing to consider what you've done and how it's affected, you may better comprehend your shortcomings, strengths, and opportunities for improvement.

Secondly, reflection on action builds resilience. Unavoidably, there will be obstacles and disappointments in our path. But by reflecting on these experiences, we learn how to bounce back stronger and more resilient than before. We develop the ability to adapt and overcome obstacles with grace and determination.

Making better decisions is yet another important advantage. You may make better judgements in the future by thinking back on your previous decisions and how they turned out. You gain knowledge from your achievements and mistakes, which enables you to face new tasks with assurance and clarity.

Thus, as young leaders, how can we make reflection on action a part of our everyday lives? The first step is to schedule a specific time for introspection. This might be a weekly gathering for the team to talk about the latest experiences and initiatives. Alternatively, it may be a personal writing routine in which you jot down ideas and discoveries.

It's also important to create a supportive environment for reflection. Encourage your team members to share their reflections openly and without judgment. Celebrate successes and learn from challenges together as a team.

For young leaders, reflection on action is an effective technique. It's about pausing, reflecting, and drawing lessons from our past. Adopting this approach may help us cultivate a culture of development, adaptability, and ongoing progress in both our teams and ourselves. Therefore, let's commit to taking account of our activities for the benefit of the people we lead as well as for ourselves. We can develop into tomorrow's perceptive and influential leaders by working together.

Chapter 6

The Leadership Equation: Comfort, Space,
and Recognition

In the delicate interplay of leadership, there is a fine balance between comfort, space, and recognition. These elements weave together to form what I have come to understand as The Leadership Equation. It is a formula not bound by rigid rules, but rather a fluid philosophy that guides effective leadership. As I reflect on my experiences, particularly those at the Gandhi Fellowship assessment centre in 2019, during an interview at Jagriti in 2023, and conversations with Mr Vishwas Pandey, Associate Director in JECP, I find that each of these incidents reflects the essence of this equation.

Comfort: The Power of Making Others Comfortable
&
Recognition: Unveiling Hidden Leadership

In 2019, I found myself in a profound lesson in leadership without even realizing it. The setting was the assessment centre of the Gandhi Fellowship in Assam, Guwahati. It was a standard hotel hall, and about 25 of us, all young and eager, were seated in a circle. Yet, despite our shared purpose, an uncomfortable silence hung in the air. Conversations were hesitant, and interactions seemed stilted.

Then, like a breath of fresh air, a Naga boy entered the room. He exuded warmth and genuine interest as he went around the circle, saying hello to each of us. Instantly, the atmosphere transformed. The tension vanished, and a noticeable feeling of comfort and friendship took its place. It was a simple act, yet its impact was profound. At that moment, I realised the power of making others comfortable.

Space: Empowering Through Freedom

Fast forward to 2023, and I found myself seated in an interview at Jagriti, facing Mr. Anurag, the Chief Operating Officer (COO). Eager to understand the organisation's approach to leadership, I posed a question about the space provided to employees. How much room was given for individuality and creativity within the framework of achieving targets?

Mr. Anurag's response was nothing short of enlightening. "We have targets," he began, his voice measured yet brimming with assurance, "but to fulfil these, you are free to use your style." It was a liberating statement, emphasising the importance of space within the organisational structure. The idea that employees were trusted to find their path to success within the broader objectives of the organisation was empowering.

This notion of space was further reinforced when I joined Jagriti and had the opportunity to observe Mr Vishwas Pandey, the leader of the organisation, in action. He was not a distant figure in a corner office but a presence on the ground, actively engaged with the team. During one of our conversations, I asked him about his views on leadership.
"What do you think makes a leader?" I inquired, curious to hear his insights. Mr Pandey, with his characteristic thoughtfulness, paused before responding. "I might be incorrect," he began, "but I feel leaders give space to people to work and simultaneously guide their team."

His words struck a chord within me, resonating with the principles of The Leadership Equation. Leaders, it seemed, were not just taskmasters or visionaries. They were facilitators of growth, providing the necessary space for individuals to flourish while offering guidance and support along the way.

This conversation with Mr. Pandey brought to mind a poignant example from my past. In college, there was a brilliant girl, who even outshined me in academics. However, she was introverted, preferring the quiet corners of the classroom to the spotlight of leadership roles. I, on the other hand, was more extroverted and equally capable.

Yet, when it came time to choose a class representative, I was the one selected, not her. At the time, it seemed natural - the outgoing, vocal student taking on a leadership role. However, Mr. Pandey's words made me rethink this assumption. Could it be that we often overlook the quieter, more introspective individuals who possess equal if not greater leadership potential?

This reflection led me to a deeper understanding of recognition within The Leadership Equation. It is not just about acknowledging those who are outwardly visible or vocal. True recognition means unveiling hidden talents and potential, and giving credit where it is due, even if it comes from unexpected sources.

As I weave together these threads of comfort, space, and recognition, I see the textile of leadership taking shape. Effective leaders, like Mr. Anurag and Mr. Pandey & leaders around us understand the importance of creating a comfortable environment where individuals can thrive. They provide the necessary space for growth and creativity, trusting their team members to find their unique paths to success.

Moreover, they have a keen eye for recognizing potential, even in the most unexpected places. By embracing these elements of The Leadership Equation, they foster a culture of empowerment and growth within their organisations.

In my journey, these experiences have left an indelible mark. They have shaped my understanding of leadership, guiding me to strive for a balance of comfort, space, and recognition in my interactions with others. As I continue to learn and grow, I carry with me the lessons gleaned from these moments, knowing that they form the foundation of effective leadership in any setting.

Chapter 7

Leading with Emotional Intelligence

In today's workplaces, being a great leader isn't just about making big decisions or giving orders. It's also about understanding and managing emotions – both yours and your team's. This is where Emotional Intelligence (EI) comes in. EI is like a superpower for leaders, helping them navigate tough situations with empathy, compassion, and resilience.

Understanding Emotions

Let's start with understanding emotions. Emotions are those feelings that bubble up inside of us. They can be happy, sad, angry, or even anxious. As a leader, it's crucial to recognize and acknowledge your own emotions. Take a moment to ask yourself, "How am I feeling right now?" This self-awareness is the first step in developing emotional intelligence.

Managing Emotions

Once you're aware of your emotions, the next step is managing them. Imagine you're feeling frustrated about a project not going as planned. Instead of lashing out or hiding your feelings, pause and take a deep breath. This pause gives you the space to choose how to respond. Maybe you decide to talk calmly with your team to brainstorm solutions. That's managing your emotions in action.

Empathy and Compassion

Now, let's talk about empathy and compassion. Empathy is putting yourself in someone else's shoes, and understanding how they feel. Compassion is taking that understanding and wanting to help. As a leader, empathy means truly listening to your team members. It's about hearing not just their words but also their emotions. When someone is struggling, a compassionate leader offers support and encouragement, showing they care about the person, not just the work.

Resilience and Stress Management

Leading can be tough, with deadlines, conflicts, and challenges piling up. But that's where resilience comes in. It's like a mental muscle that helps you bounce back from setbacks. Think of it as a trampoline – when tough situations come your way, resilience helps you bounce back up instead of staying down. Building resilience means finding simple, healthy ways to cope with stress. It could be walking, talking to a friend, or practising mindfulness. These little breaks recharge your batteries and keep you strong for the next challenge.

Putting it into Practice

Let's imagine a scenario: A team member, Sarah, is feeling overwhelmed with her workload. As a leader with emotional intelligence, here's how you might handle it:

- First, you notice Sarah seems stressed during a team meeting.
- You approach her after the meeting and ask, "Hey Sarah you seemed a bit stressed. Is everything okay?"
- Sarah opens up about her workload and feeling overwhelmed.
- Instead of dismissing her concerns, you listen with empathy. "I hear you, Sarah. It sounds like you've got a lot on your plate."
- Then, you offer support and solutions. "Let's work together to prioritise your tasks. And if you need extra help, I'm here for you."

By developing emotional intelligence, we create a positive work environment where people feel heard, supported, and motivated.

Therefore, keep in mind the power of emotional intelligence the next time you are presented with a challenging circumstance. It may certainly make all the difference in becoming an exceptional leader.

Chapter 8

Collaboration and Inclusivity: Fostering a Culture of Belonging

Collaboration and inclusivity are the keys to creating a workplace where everyone feels valued and respected. In today's diverse and interconnected world, businesses are recognizing the immense power of bringing together individuals from various backgrounds and perspectives. Onboarding diversity and inclusion isn't just the right thing to do; it's also a smart business strategy. When we embrace different viewpoints and experiences, we open ourselves up to a world of new ideas, creativity, and innovation.

Bringing diversity is about more than just hiring people from different backgrounds; it's about creating an environment where everyone feels welcome and valued. This means celebrating the unique qualities and perspectives that each person brings to the table. Whether it's cultural diversity, different life experiences, or varying ways of thinking, diversity enriches our teams and helps us see things from a new angle on the other than inclusion, is about ensuring that everyone has a seat at the table and a voice that is heard. It's about creating a sense of belonging where individuals feel respected and valued for who they are, regardless of their background or identity. Inclusivity can also be created:

1. *Collaboration Across Teams and Departments*

Effective collaboration isn't just about working together within our teams; it's about breaking down silos and fostering connections across departments. When we bring together individuals with diverse expertise and perspectives, we create a melting pot of ideas and solutions. Collaboration allows us to tap into the collective intelligence of the entire organisation, leading to better decision-making and innovative solutions. However, building cross-departmental collaboration requires intentional efforts. Leaders play a crucial role in facilitating these connections by creating opportunities for teams to unite, share knowledge, and work towards common goals.

2. *Building a Culture of Belonging*

At the heart of collaboration and inclusivity lies the concept of belonging. A culture of belonging is one where everyone feels accepted, respected, and valued for who they are. It's about creating an environment where people can bring their whole selves to work without fear of judgement or exclusion. When employees feel they belong, they are more engaged, motivated, and committed to the organisation's success. Building this culture starts with leadership, setting the tone from the top down that inclusivity and belonging are not just nice-to-haves but integral to the company's culture and values. The conscious practice of a non-judgemental attitude is required to celebrate each failure and success.

3. *Practical Steps for Creating Inclusivity and Collaboration*

Creating a culture of collaboration and inclusivity requires intentional efforts and ongoing commitment. Here are some practical steps that leaders and organisations can take:

a). Lead by Example: Leaders should demonstrate inclusivity in their actions, decisions, and interactions. They should actively seek out diverse perspectives and show respect for differing opinions.

b). Establish Open Communication: Create open and honest communication channels where team members feel safe expressing their ideas, concerns, and feedback. Encourage regular dialogue and feedback sessions. When a team is giving feedback it should also be a choice of an individual to keep it confidential or open.

c). Promote Diversity in Hiring: Ensure that hiring practices promote diversity by removing biases and barriers. Implement diverse recruitment strategies to attract a wide range of candidates.

d). Provide Diversity and Inclusion Training: Offer training programs and workshops on diversity, equity, and inclusion. Educate employees on unconscious biases and how to create an inclusive workplace.

e). Facilitate Cross-Functional Collaboration: Organise cross-departmental meetings, projects, or task forces to encourage collaboration and knowledge sharing. Create opportunities for employees from different teams to work together.

f). Recognize and Celebrate Diversity: Celebrate diverse holidays, cultural traditions, and achievements within the organisation. Acknowledge the contributions of individuals from diverse backgrounds.

g). Create a sharing leadership Environment: I met
Mr Rajesh Kachroo at Drishtee Foundation he
taught me how shared leadership among team
members gives you an understanding and
importance of the person working in a position.
This also helps you to enhance your capacity and
boost your confidence.

Chapter 9

Self-care as leader

In the fast-paced world of leadership, taking care of oneself often takes a back seat to the demands of the job. However, the truth is that effective leadership starts with a healthy and balanced leader. The importance of self-care in leadership cannot be overstated. When leaders prioritise their well-being, they not only perform better but also set a positive example for their teams.

Imagine a car trying to run on an empty tank - it's bound to break down eventually. Similarly, leaders who neglect their well-being risk burnout decreased productivity, and compromised decision-making. It's like trying to pour from an empty cup; sooner or later, there's nothing left to give. Realising this, many successful leaders have emphasised the need for self-care. Take the example of Arianna Huffington, founder of The Huffington Post. After collapsing from exhaustion, she made self-care a priority, recognizing that success means little without health and well-being.

Maintaining balance as a leader is all about finding what works best for you. It's not about adding more to your plate but rather about prioritising what truly matters. Start by carving out time for activities that recharge your batteries, whether it's spending time with loved ones, exercising, or simply taking a moment to breathe. Look at Richard Branson, founder of the Virgin Group; he's known for his adventurous spirit and makes time for kite-surfing and other activities he loves, which helps him stay energised and focused in his leadership role.

Your mental and physical health are the foundation of your leadership. Just as you wouldn't expect a computer to function without regular maintenance, your body and mind need care too. Leaders like Oprah Winfrey have spoken openly about the importance of mental health. She practises mindfulness and meditation to stay centred and grounded amidst the demands of her career. Additionally, prioritising physical health through regular exercise and a balanced diet not only boosts energy but also enhances cognitive function, enabling better decision-making.

Story

Consider the story of Mark, a high-powered executive who was always on the go. He prided himself on working long hours and never taking breaks. However, this lifestyle eventually caught up with him. Mark started experiencing constant fatigue, irritability, and a decline in performance. It wasn't until he hit a breaking point and had to take time off for health reasons that he realised the importance of self-care. Upon returning, Mark made changes to his routine. He started taking short breaks throughout the day to recharge, prioritise sleep, and make time for hobbies he enjoyed. Not only did his health improve, but he also found that his leadership abilities flourished.

Similarly, Sarah, a manager in a fast-paced tech company, found herself overwhelmed with deadlines and responsibilities. She often skipped meals and worked late into the night. This led to increased stress and anxiety, impacting her relationships and work performance. After seeking advice from a mentor, Sarah learned to set boundaries and prioritise self-care. She started scheduling regular breaks during her workday, practised mindfulness exercises, and made time for hobbies outside of work. As a result, Sarah found that she was more focused, productive, and happier both at work and in her personal life.

In conclusion, self-care is not a luxury reserved for those with extra time; it's a necessity for effective leadership. By prioritising your well-being, you not only enhance your performance but also set a positive example for your team. Just as a well-maintained car runs smoothly, a well-cared-for leader leads with clarity, resilience, and inspiration. So, take a page from successful leaders who prioritise self-care, and remember: you can't pour from an empty cup. Take care of yourself first, and watch as your leadership and impact grow.

Chapter 10

Leaders are not ordinary, they make Extraordinary choices

Leaders aren't just those big names you see in the news or on social media. They're the ones who make the cool, bold moves that shake things up. What makes them stand out? It's not just being there; it's the epic choices they make when things get tough.

Think about it – leaders have to be brave. They're faced with tons of options, each with its risks and rewards. It's like a video game where you have to choose your next move carefully, except this game is real life! Leaders like Elon Musk and Malala Yousafzai didn't settle for the easy path. Nope, they went for the crazy ideas and made them work. Elon with his electric cars at Tesla, and Malala fighting for girls' education – these folks saw a chance to change the world and went for it.

When things go haywire, that's when leaders shine. Picture a superhero staying calm in the middle of chaos. During COVID-19, leaders had to make tough calls every day, from lockdowns to mask mandates. Their choices weren't just about keeping people safe but saving lives.

But it's not just about making the right call. It's about sticking to your values too. Leaders like Nelson Mandela and Mahatma Gandhi showed us that. Mandela chose forgiveness over revenge, and Gandhi led India to independence with peaceful protests. These weren't just smart moves; they were about doing what's right.

And let's not forget – leaders don't do it alone. They build teams, inspire others, and share the load. By giving people power and responsibility, they make sure their impact lasts long after they're gone.

So, if you ever wonder what sets leaders apart, it's those epic choices they make. They're not just there to fill a seat; they're there to shake things up and make the world better. As we go through life's challenges, let's remember – leaders aren't just extra; they're the ones making the big moves that push us all forward.

Have you heard this song by Michael Jackson?

We could fly so high
Let our spirits never die
In my heart, I feel you are all my brothers
Create a world with no fear

"Heal the World" by Michael Jackson aligns with extraordinary leadership, where leaders make choices beyond the ordinary. The song's call for unity and compassion reflects leaders who envision a better world and inspire positive change. It emphasizes empathy, urging leaders to prioritize the well-being of others. Like the song's message of creating a better place for future generations, extraordinary leaders focus on leaving a positive legacy. "Heal the World" is an anthem for this kind of leadership, reminding us of our power to make a difference. It's about choosing kindness, inspiring others, and working together to heal our world.

Chapter 11

I don't know

I met Mamta Mam at Drishtee Foundation, and let me tell you, she's around 70 years old but radiates this youthful energy that's truly inspiring. Mamta Mam, Satyan Mishra's mother and President of the Drishtee Foundation, shows up at the office every single day, ready to tackle new challenges. What's even more amazing is her attitude towards learning. I've seen her a couple of times feeling stuck and not sure about something, but she's never shy to say, "Can you help me with this? I'm not sure how to do it." Now, that's real courage and humility right there!

I've been lucky to work alongside Mamta Mam for about a year, and her eagerness to learn is just remarkable. She's always open to new ideas and approaches, and her humility when it comes to learning from others is truly inspiring. I've heard stories from fellow employees about how she creates this environment of trust and collaboration, where everyone feels valued and encouraged to share their knowledge.

Sundar Pichai, the CEO of Google, once said, "I'm not an expert on everything, but I'm learning." Isn't that amazing? Here's this big-shot CEO, leading one of the world's most innovative companies, and he openly admits that he's still learning. It's a powerful message that even those at the top are humble enough to seek knowledge and grow.

So, whether it's Mamta Mam at Drishtee Foundation or Sundar Pichai at Google, these leaders teach us an invaluable lesson: it's all about being open to learning, no matter where you are in your career. They show us the importance of humility, curiosity, and the willingness to ask for help when needed. And for that, we are truly grateful to have such inspiring leaders guiding the way.

This version aims to connect the stories of Mamta Mishra and Sundar Pichai in an informal, grateful tone for young adults, highlighting their humility, eagerness to learn, and the positive impact they have on creating a culture of learning and collaboration.

In my professional journey, I've had the privilege of working with three remarkable organisations - Piramal Foundation, Drishtee Foundation, and Jagriti Enterprise Centre for Purvanchal. Each of these organizations fostered an environment where team members could openly admit, "I don't know. Can you help me?" This culture of openness and support was particularly evident during presentations at Jagriti Enterprise Centre for Purvanchal. In our presentations, we had a designated column for seeking support, whether it be from the Founder or a senior reporting manager. This practice encouraged a collaborative approach, where no question was too small or a problem too big to seek help for. Additionally, there were separate avenues, such as calls, to check if anyone was feeling stuck or needed assistance. I am grateful for the experiences I've had in these organizations, where leaders led by example and inspired a culture of mutual support and growth.

Chapter 12

Freedom to Fail

When I attended an Induction at PSL (Piram School of Learning), something called 'Freedom to Fail' was introduced to us. It was a whole new idea for me. During this program, the fellows were asking questions about the challenges we might face, like failures, language barriers, food issues, and how we would manage everything. There were a lot of questions from the fellows, and the facilitator's response surprised me: "You are free to fail and learn."

This was quite surprising because, growing up, we often hear from our parents and relatives that we must always strive to come first. But really, how can all 60 students in a class of 60 come first? It's a puzzling concept.

In many schools and colleges, the pressure to excel and be the best is immense. We are often told that being first is the only way to succeed. This mentality can be stressful and sometimes unrealistic. It creates a sense of competition that may not always be healthy.

However, at PSL, they had a different perspective. They emphasised the importance of learning through failures. The idea of 'Freedom to Fail' means it's okay to make mistakes. It's okay not to be perfect all the time. Instead of fearing failure, we were encouraged to embrace it as a part of the learning process.

This approach makes a lot of sense. In the real world, we will face challenges, we will stumble, and we will make mistakes. It's how we grow and learn from these experiences that truly matters. By allowing ourselves the freedom to fail, we open doors to valuable lessons and personal growth.

In a class of 60 students, expecting each one to come first is unrealistic. Each person has their strengths and weaknesses. We are all unique individuals with different abilities and talents. It's important to acknowledge this diversity and celebrate it.

So, the idea of 'Freedom to Fail' at PSL was refreshing. It taught us that it's okay not to be perfect. It's okay to try new things, even if we might fail at first. What's important is that we learn from these failures and use them as stepping stones towards success.

The concept of 'Freedom to Fail' challenges the traditional notion of always striving to be first. It encourages us to embrace failure as a part of learning and growth. It's a liberating idea that allows us to explore, experiment, and ultimately, become better versions of ourselves.

The time I have understood what it means you are free to fail in an organisation or any company if the culture allows you to experiment and learn and that's the best organisation where the leader works the Leader creates and the Leader build. If you're an organisation or a company, don't give yourself a space to experiment. Don't allow yourself to use your mind your working with the boss and they're Breaking your power to visualise things out of the box and this will not help you to flourish as a leader.

When I finally grasped the idea of being free to fail in a company, it clicked for me. The best organizations are the ones where leaders encourage experimentation and learning. They're the ones where leaders aren't just bosses, but creators and builders of something great.

But if you're in a company that doesn't let you try new things, it's like working with a boss who holds you back. They limit your ability to think creatively and outside the box. This kind of environment won't help you grow as a leader. You're in a job where your boss only wants things done their way. They won't let you suggest new ideas or try different approaches. It feels stifling, right? That's not the kind of place where leaders thrive.

On the other side of the coin, is a company where your leader says, "Go ahead, give it a shot. If it doesn't work out, we'll learn from it." That's the kind of environment where leaders can truly shine. It's a place where mistakes aren't seen as failures but as opportunities to learn and improve.

In organisations that embrace the freedom to fail, there's room to experiment, to think creatively, and to take risks. Leaders in these companies understand that growth comes from trying new things, even if they don't always work out.

So, if you're thinking about your future career, remember this: Look for organisations that value innovation and learning. Seek out leaders who encourage you to think outside the box and aren't afraid of a few bumps along the way.

Being free to fail isn't about messing up on purpose. It's about having the freedom to explore new ideas, to push boundaries, and to learn from both successes and failures. That's the kind of environment where leaders flourish and where you can truly make a difference.

Recollecting

The choices you make are not only coincidental events; rather, they are a reflection of your abilities, mindset, and social circles. Care and imagination are the paintbrush colours that create the most exquisite images on the canvas of life. It would be a lonely world if people didn't give a damn about one other's welfare. Likewise, if we didn't dare to dream and visualise a better future, progress would stagnate. Take the incredible journey of Jagriti Yatra, the world's largest train journey, for example. It started with a vision, and a dream to inspire change, and it became a reality through action and care for the community.

You will meet leaders who don't pursue fame or a place in history as you go further into the chapters of life. Rather, they change lives—beginning with their own. Gratitude serves as a daily energiser against negativity and a constant reminder of blessings. While a boss could enjoy comparisons and rivalry, a good leader understands that inclusion and teamwork are essential for success. They provide forums where all voices are heard, promoting a culture of development and cooperation.

Being a leader involves more than simply going forward; it also involves looking back. The mirror of reflection allows us to see ourselves, grow from our failures, and celebrate our victories. A leader's biggest asset is their humility; they don't hesitate to acknowledge when they don't know something. They know that self-care is the foundation of genuine leadership. Leaders take care of themselves so they may take care of others, much like a gardener takes care of their garden.

Every single one of you can lead. It is about the decisions you make daily, not about a title or a position of power. Every choice you make, no matter how tiny, has an impact on both your life and the environment. Accept the risk and have the guts to make remarkable decisions that inspire, motivate, and bring about change. The world is waiting for your special insights, your new viewpoints, and your persistent faith in an improved future.

Leadership success is a journey, not a destination. A leader carries humble behaviour, extraordinary actions and a collaborative attitude. It's about making decisions that are consistent with your mission, beliefs, and interests. Be brave in your thinking, kind in your deeds, and strong in the face of difficulty. You all have the power to shape the future, and I am confident that you will all leave a lasting impression on the globe. So, with grace, honesty, and the understanding that you can change things, go out, my young leaders. The most important thing is to keep experimenting with your choices, you will learn with each choice.

Reference

- Smith, J. (2020). The Power of Thank You: How Gratitude Can Enhance Workplace Culture. Harvard Business Review.

- Jones, R., et al. (2018). Gratitude in Leadership: A Study of Its Impact on Trust in Teams. Journal of Personality and Social Psychology.

- Chen, L., et al. (2019). The Role of Gratitude in Organisational Culture: Implications for Employee Well-Being. Journal of Applied Psychology.

- Garcia, M. (2017). Leading with Gratitude: Building Resilience in Times of Challenge. Journal of Business Ethics.
- Grant, A. M., & Gino, F. (2010). A little thanks goes a long way: Explaining why gratitude expressions motivate prosocial behaviour. Journal of Personality and Social Psychology, 98(6), 946–955.
- Emmons, R. A., & McCullough, M. E. (2003). Counting blessings versus burdens: An experimental investigation of gratitude and subjective well-being in daily life. Journal of Personality and Social Psychology, 84(2), 377–389.
- **Harvard Business School Online:**

- ○ Reflective Leadership: The Power of Self-Awareness
- **The Leader Boy**:
  - ○ The Art of Reflective Leadership
- **Forbes**:
  - ○ Why Reflective Leadership Is Essential for Future-Ready Organizations
- Cox, T. (1994). Cultural Diversity in Organisations: Theory, Research, and Practice. San Francisco, CA: Berrett-Koehler Publishers.
- Greenberg, J. (2003). Diversity in the Workplace: Benefits, Challenges, and the Required Managerial Tools. Journal of Managerial Psychology, 18(4), 18-32.
- Herring, C. (2009). Does Diversity Pay?: Race, Gender, and the Business Case for Diversity. American Sociological Review, 74(2), 208-224.
- Shore, L. M., Randel, A. E., Chung, B. G., Dean, M. A., Holcombe Ehrhart, K., & Singh, G. (2011). Inclusion and Diversity in Work Groups: A Review and Model for Future Research. Journal of Management, 37(4), 1262-1289.
- Thomas, R. R. Jr. (1999). Diversity as Strategy. Harvard Business Review, 77(2), 98-108.
- Uhl-Bien, M., & Marion, R. (2008). Complexity Leadership in Bureaucratic Forms of Organizing: A Muddling Through

Perspective. Advances in Strategic Management, 25, 297-323.
- Williams, K. Y., & O'Reilly, C. A. III. (1998). Demography and Diversity in Organisations: A Review of 40 Years of Research. Research in Organisational Behaviour, 20, 77-140.
- OpenAi

Let's Connect